KU-070-798

I celebrated World Book Day 2022
with this gift from my local bookseller
and Hachette Children's Group

*This one's for all the teachers
and support staff out there.
You're LEGENDS, all of you.
Thank you for everything you do.*

WORLD BOOK DAY

World Book Day's mission is to offer every child and young person the opportunity to read and love books by giving you the chance to have a book of your own.

To find out more, and for fun activities including our monthly book club, video stories and book recommendations visit worldbookday.com

World Book Day is a charity funded by publishers and booksellers in the UK and Ireland.

World Book Day is also made possible by generous sponsorship from National Book Tokens and support from authors and illustrators.

First published in Great Britain in 2022 by Wren & Rook
Text copyright © Rashmi Sirdeshpande 2022
Design copyright © Hodder & Stoughton Limited 2022
All rights reserved.

The right of Rashmi Sirdeshpande to be identified as the author of this Work has been
asserted by them in accordance with the Copyright, Designs & Patents Act 1988.

ISBN: 978 1 5263 6440 1
Export ISBN: 978 1 5263 6451 7
1 3 5 7 9 10 8 6 4 2

Wren & Rook
An imprint of
Hachette Children's Group
Part of Hodder & Stoughton
Carmelite House
50 Victoria Embankment
London EC4Y 0DZ

An Hachette UK Company
www.hachette.co.uk
www.hachettechildrens.co.uk

Printed and bound in and bound in Great Britain by Clays Ltd, Elcograf S.p.A

The website addresses (URLs) included in this book were valid at the time of going to press.
However, it is possible that contents or addresses may have changed since the publication
of this book. No responsibility for any such changes can be accepted by either the author or
the publisher.

Velcro ® is a registered trademark of Velcro BVBA. LEGO ® is a registered trademark of
LEGO Juris A/S. Play-Doh ® is a registered trademark of Hasbro, Inc. Slinky. McDonald's ®
is a registered trademark of McDonald's International Property Company, Ltd. Barbie ®
is a registered trademark of Mattel, Inc. Harley Davidson ® is a registered trademark of
H-D U.S.A., LLC. WhatsApp ® is a registered trademark of WhatsApp LLC. Facebook ® is a
registered trademark of Facebook, Inc. BearHugs ® is a registered trademark of Faye Savory.
The Big Issue ® is a registered trademark of The Big Issue Group Limited. Infarm ® is a
registered trademark of Infarm Indoor Urban Farming. Apple ® is a registered trademark
of Apple Inc. Google ® is a registered trademark of Google LLC. Netflix ® is a registered
trademark of Netflix, Inc. Nintendo ® is a registered trademark of Nintendo Co., Ltd.
YouTube ® is a registered trademark of Google LLC.

THINK LIKE A BOSS

Discover the skills that turn

great ideas into **CASH**

BY RASHMI SIRDESHPANDE

ILLUSTRATED BY ADAM HAYES

wren
&rook

CONTENTS

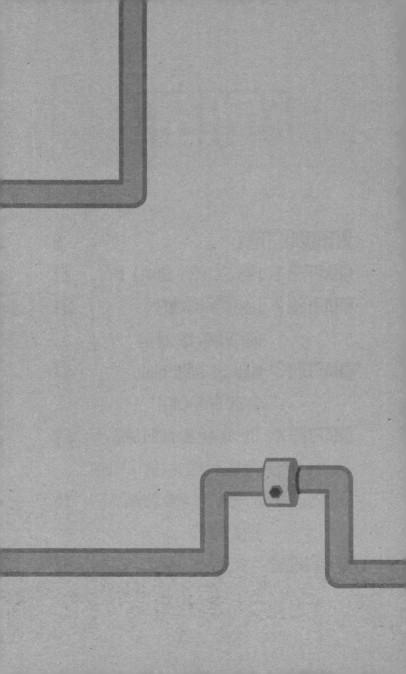

INTRODUCTION

BIG SHOT

BOSS

INVENTOR

Who pops into your head when you see these words? Maybe it's Steve Jobs and Steve Wozniak, co-founders of Apple Inc. Or Elon Musk making electric cars and spacecraft. Or talk show host and TV producer Oprah Winfrey. Maybe it's even the people you know in your local community – such as those who run the local corner shop, the bookshop and the gym. But have you ever considered that *you* could become a boss? Yes, you!

BUSINESS PERSON

TYCOON

INNOVATOR

Though you might think making money is just for adults, or that business sounds *really* complicated and inventing stuff is just for super clever people, here's a secret: anyone can be a boss! And it's actually much easier than you think …

THE BOSS

Think about all the things you use at home or at school:

* **GLUE**
* **CARTONS AND TIN CANS TO KEEP FOOD AND DRINKS FRESH**
* **SOAPS, SHAMPOOS AND TOOTHPASTE**
* **LIGHT BULBS**
* **PHONES**
* **TOILETS!**

Someone invented these. They saw an opportunity to improve things or they came across an interesting discovery by accident and turned it into something useful. Swiss engineer George de Mestral got the idea for Velcro when the prickly seeds from a burdock plant kept sticking to his trousers and his dog's fur when he was out in the Alps. Later on,

Velcro would even be used by *astronauts* to secure things like food and equipment up in space!

Some inventions can even change lives. Ever heard of 'Braille'? *Fifteen-year-old* Louis Braille invented this clever writing system in 1824. It's based on raised dots and helps visually impaired people (like Louis!) read and write. More recently, a girl called Gitanjali Rao developed a low-cost device to detect contaminated drinking water. She first started working on the idea when she was eleven years old. Yep, *eleven*!

These young inventors have one big thing in common. They saw a problem, they were determined to DO something about it and they transformed a great idea into a reality. They were able to think like *entrepreneurs*.

An entrepreneur is someone who comes up with an idea or invention and uses it to start a business. When they're faced with a challenge, a great entrepreneur can think creatively and spot stuff that other people might miss.

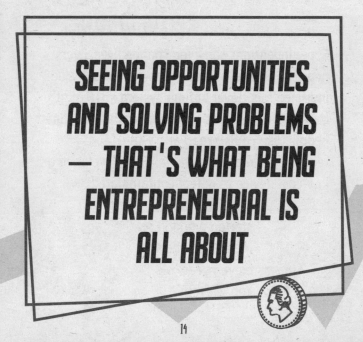

SEEING OPPORTUNITIES AND SOLVING PROBLEMS — THAT'S WHAT BEING ENTREPRENEURIAL IS ALL ABOUT

THINK LIKE A BOSS

'Most people keep their heads fixed in position, looking straight at the same world. But by tilting your head, things appear different. And you ask questions like: what if this mug is really a plant pot? You are now being creative. The lesson? Always tilt your head' – **DHRUPAD KARWA, founder of HaikuJAM, a group poetry-writing app**

But *why* do people set up businesses? Well, for all kinds of reasons:

- To make some CASH. KER-CHINNNG
- To be their own BOSS
- To be CREATIVE – making things, fixing things and finding solutions to challenges
- To use their skills to do something they LOVE
- To do some GOOD in the world

For some people, it's a mix of these reasons. Maybe even all of them! Do any of these things sound good to you? Well, you definitely don't have to be a grown-up to do all this cool stuff. This could be **YOU** now, bossing it, getting creative, doing what you love and maybe even making a difference while you're at it. And possibly turning that creativity into **CASH**.

 But it's not *just* about the money. It's not *even* about setting up a business! Because here's the thing …

You can still *think* like an entrepreneur and **BOSS IT** at life, whatever you do. This doesn't mean walking around thinking you're the best thing since sliced bread and acting like you own the place.

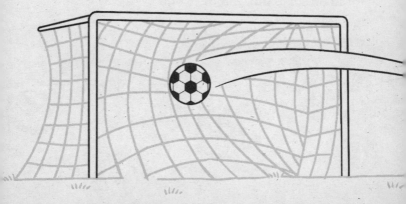

It means approaching life like a **BOSS** – being creative and confident, and imaginatively solving problems that come your way. It's about understanding money and being savvy with how you spend it (and how you save it!). And it's about having the courage to try new things and not being afraid to fail.

So if you picked up this book, but you don't have a big business idea and you're wondering if all this is really for you – **HELLO, YES, IT TOTALLY IS.** Because once you have that **BOSS** mindset, you can use it in *all* areas of *your* life, whether that's at school, in sports or to find fantastic ways to do some good in the world. It means you can get creative and explore new things without worrying tooooo much about making mistakes. It means you can tackle any problem or task that is thrown your way with cool confidence. And you can have some serious fun while you're at it too.

Here's what we're going to do. First, we'll do a quick introduction to money, because that's something all bosses need to get to grips with. Next, we'll dream up a fantastic fantasy business idea – small and sneaky or big and bold, it's up to you! *Then,* we'll figure out how that fantasy business can actually *make some money.* Along the way, we'll meet some amazing entrepreneurs who have a wise word or two to share, and we'll pick up a 'magical briefcase' packed with all the spells and potions you need to get set up for **SUCCESS.** Last – but *totally* not least – we'll look at how *real* bosses use all that boss magic to do some **GOOD** in the world.

WHAT DO YOU THINK? Are you up for building a boss mindset and discovering how great ideas are turned into **CASH**? Well, in that case, we've got a **LOT** to get through, so we better get cracking …

CHAPTER 1
FIRST STOP –
MONEY 101

I said it's not *just* about the money, but money's pretty important.

If you're going to be a hotshot business tycoon, you need to understand it. Actually, scrap that. **WHATEVER** you do, you need to understand money. Whether we're talking about coins and notes, bank cards or cash sitting in a bank account, money pays for things like food, clothes and somewhere to call home. And it lets us buy the nice things we've got our eye on. Someone will be taking care of this stuff for you today, but one day that'll be *your* job. So it's worth making sure you've nailed the basics!

Now, you might not have very much money at all right now. And that's **OK**. You can still think like a boss and you can definitely still shine as an entrepreneur. The best entrepreneurs are *scrappy* – in the business world this means that they're very good at getting by with very little. We'll come back to this in chapter 4.

BOSSES START WITH WHATEVER THEY HAVE AND THEY TAKE IT ONE STEP AT A TIME.

That's what Omari McQueen did. Omari's dad taught him and his big brother to cook so they could help out at home when their mum was really unwell. For Omari, it turned into a real passion. By the age of twelve he had started a vegan dips business, opened a vegan Caribbean pop-up restaurant and published his own cookbook. Now, he even has his own vegan cookery show on children's TV channel CBBC. I mean, **WOW**.

Omari may be doing amazing things today but it all started in his kitchen, using the stuff he had at home. That's true for so many entrepreneurs. You have to start *somewhere*, right? But *wherever* you start and whatever you do, you're going to need to deal with money. So before we get down to business **(SEE WHAT I DID THERE?)**, let's quickly talk about **CASH.**

FIVE THINGS TO REMEMBER ABOUT MONEY

1 RESPECT IT. TAKE CARE OF IT. If you remember how precious It is and the power it has, you'll make good decisions. Because … *why wouldn't you?*
Speaking of good decisions …

2 BE A SAVVY SPENDER. It's tempting to splash your cash when you get hold of some. But don't. Received some money as a gift? Hit pause. Think about how to spend it.

Watch out for tricksy advertising making you think you need stuff you don't need or making you think something's an **AMAZING DEAL** when it's *not*. Bosses don't fall for that stuff. Nope. They know the difference between *needs* and *wants*.

3 BE A SNEAKY SAVER. When you get hold of some money, get into the habit of setting a bit aside. Some people call this 'saving for a rainy day'. You might want to save *for* something too – like those trainers on your wish list. Yes, it takes patience to save. But it's worth it. It's a habit so many grown-ups wish they'd started earlier. So consider this a head start!

4 IF YOU GET IT, GIVE IT. There are so many things that need fixing in the world.

We don't all get the same start and the same chances in life, and things can change so quickly for any one of us. Our planet's in serious need of some care and attention too. So if you're lucky enough to have some cash to spare one day, you might want to think about *sharing* it and spending it on a cause you care about. Every little bit helps.

27

5 MONEY'S IMPORTANT BUT IT'S NOT EVERYTHING.

You need money for food, clothes, a place to live and for some of the nice things you want too (*lots* of them, even! Why not?!). But once the basics are taken care of, as *cheesy* as it is, the best things in life really are free.

28

FRIENDSHIP

FAMILY

HAPPY
MEMORIES

NATURE

 LAUGHTER

Successful entrepreneurs always keep these things in mind. They respect money. They're savvy spenders and sneaky savers. And true bosses? They're givers too. They know how to manage their money but they also know there's sooooo much more to life. Now you have the basics under your belt too. Ready to get back to business? **OK, LET'S GO.**

CHAPTER 2
FANTASY
BUSINESS -
DREAMING
UP IDEAS

If you could set up a business – **ANY** business – what would it be? Have you ever thought about it? Well, now's your chance. Let's play **FANTASY BUSINESS**. As you read this book, get thinking about a business idea. It can be as wild or as practical as you like. Now, you might be thinking, *Hang on, I don't have any ideas*. That's OK. Follow the steps below and let your brain loose to do some creative thinking. And if you *still* don't have any ideas – don't worry, there are tips here to help set you up for success no matter what you do. Plus, we're going to meet some pretty cool business bosses to inspire us along the way!

STEP 1 FIND A PROBLEM TO SOLVE

You can have the coolest ideas in the world but if no one wants to buy what you're selling, you're stuck. So instead of thinking about **IDEAS**, think about **PROBLEMS**.

When Callum Daniel was eight, he was desperate to learn about making and coding robots but couldn't find robotics courses for children like him. So … he set up iCodeRobots to run his own classes to teach six to twelve year olds how to make and code robots! And when eleven-year-old Lily Born invented a spill-proof cup called the Kangaroo Cup, she didn't start by saying, 'OOH, I'M GOING TO DESIGN A COOL CUP'. Lily's grandfather had Parkinson's disease, and she noticed that when he picked up a cup, his hands would often shake and his drink would spill. She thought about what might help him. *That's* how she came up with the idea for a special three-legged spill-proof cup.

So think about it: what do people *need*? What do they *want*? What would *really* make a difference? Because if you can get to the bottom of that, you've got a business idea.

HEY, WHO'S YOUR IDEAL CUSTOMER? For your fantasy business, take a moment to think about who this is. How old are they? What else do you know about them? Hobbies? Habits? Things they care about? Do you know people you can interview and test things with?

THINK LIKE A BOSS

'If you can combine something you love with helping solve a need or problem for a specific group of people, your entrepreneurial journey will be fun, fulfilling and you will soar!' – **MEI PAK, founder of Tiny Hands, a business that makes scented jewellery shaped like mini sweet treats**

STEP 2 CHECK OUT THE COMPETITION

Get ~~SNOOPING~~ RESEARCHING. Who else is out there solving this problem? Whether we're talking about people who need help cleaning their cars or people planning a party, how do they manage right now? What other companies are out there?

What do those other companies do well?
What's **MISSING?**
Take notes. **LOTS** of them.

STEP 3 COOK UP A SOLUTION

Time to come up with your own spin on things. For example, if your research shows that people find wrapping presents hard (I'm a **DISASTER** with gift wrap and sticky tape), and there's no gift-wrapping service in your area, can you create one?

Check out nine-year-old Alina Morse who started a sugar-free fruit-flavoured sweet company to solve a very specific problem. She *loved* lollipops but the standard sugary ones are *so* bad for our teeth that she teamed up with her dad to invent a healthier version called 'Zollipops'!

Back to your fantasy business. After you've checked out your competition, ask yourself these questions:
What can you do **DIFFERENTLY?**
What can you do **BETTER?**
Can you make your idea …

INCLUSIVE

FASTER

BETTER QUALITY

CHEAPER

HAND-SELECTED

HEALTHIER

HANDMADE

ENVIRONMENTALLY FRIENDLY

When you come up against any kind of problem, it's always useful to ask yourself questions. Questions help you consider things from different perspectives, and learning how *other* people do things might spark some interesting ideas in *your* brain too!

STEP 4 TEST, GET FEEDBACK, TWEAK, *REPEAT*

This bit's a cycle. Suppose you want to sell board games to help families have some screen-free fun together. First, you need to make a *prototype* – a simple, cheaper version to test. Get some feedback, tweak it and test again. Each time, it'll get better and **BETTER.**

Feedback can help you up your game with other things too – like your drawing, coding or photography skills, and even your dance moves. Can you get some feedback from a friend, a grown-up at home or a teacher? Someone who knows their stuff? It can be hard to hear sometimes – especially if there are things we can do better – but **BOSSES** know that this is a super useful stepping stone to being the *best* that you can be.

STEP 5 GET SELLINNNNNG
Think about **HOW** and **WHERE** you'd sell your fantasy product or service. Artists like Onyinye Iwu, Natelle Quek and Chris Mould sell art online. What's the best way to reach your customers? Where do they hang out? Where do they buy things? Online? A market stall? Do you need to ask anyone for permission to use a space? You'll need a grown-up to help you – would a parent, a teacher or older sibling be willing to give you a hand?

Now, when you talk about your business, *you need to tell a good story* – something that makes people sit up and listen. Think about what kind of story that will be. Is it an exciting story? A story about trust and reliability? A cosy curl-up-in-the-corner-with-a-blanket story? Think about the words and colours you'll use. Because it's ALL part of the story. In fact, grab a piece of paper and let's come up with a few things.

1 A COMPANY NAME

Make it memorable, cool, catchy and relevant.
That's what these companies did:

NIKE – the ancient Greek goddess of victory

GOOGLE – from 'googol'
– a mind-bogglingly big
number (1 and *100* zeros)

LEGO – from the Danish words
'leg godt' (which mean 'play well'!)

ACTUALLY STARTED AS A SPELLING MISTAKE

2 A LOGO

Logos are symbols that represent your business.
Like Nike's funky swoosh or the McDonald's 'M'.
They might use words or letters, shapes or
pictures, or a combination of all of these. What
logos can you think of? What ones stick in your
head? Can you design a logo for your fantasy
business? Get creative but keep it simple. No
point in a fancy complicated logo you can only
ever draw once and which no one is ever going to
remember.

3 AN ELEVATOR PITCH

Imagine you're in an elevator with a potential customer and they ask you what your business is about and what you sell. You've got thirty seconds until the elevator reaches your floor. What do you say? How do you tell your story? Your goal: to make them say **WOW, I LIKE THE SOUND OF THAT!** That's what an elevator pitch is – a short but brilliant description of your amazing idea.

STEP 6 GROW

Once you're up and running and things are going really well, you can think about **GROWING** your business. If you're selling cookies, you might start by just offering chocolate chip, and then branch out into new flavours. Or expand into new areas. Maybe you'll take over the whole **WORLD** with your cookie empire! Just imagine. What could you do with your fantasy business?

The last thing to mention here is **THE PIVOT**. To pivot is to change direction, and lots of businesses have to do it. It might be a little pivot (Netflix, for example, started by posting out rental DVDs to people, then pivoted to streaming online when they saw how popular YouTube was). But it might be a **BIG** pivot. Play-Doh started out as a wallpaper cleaner called Kutol. Nintendo tried all sorts of things from playing cards and ramen noodles to vacuum cleaners before they became the gaming sensation they are today!

43

Sometimes success takes time. And that's OK.
Sometimes things change and businesses need
to evolve as they go.

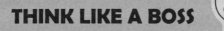

THINK LIKE A BOSS

*'Passion is the fuel you need to keep you going
during the ups and downs'* – **KATE JENKINS,
founder of Gower Cottage Brownies**

That's why **ADAPTABILITY** is such an important
skill for entrepreneurs. For **ALL** of us, in fact,
no matter what we're up to. You should see
how many times I've had to rewrite this
book! Maybe you've had to rework a drawing
too. Sometimes, even when we try our best,
things don't quite work out. And sometimes
things change unexpectedly – like having to
move house and start a new school. Suddenly
everything feels new again. Maybe even scary.
It happens. But we keep going. And we ask for
help if we need it. That's a skill too.

How did you get on with those six steps? Got an interesting fantasy business idea up your sleeve? Or the beginnings of one, maybe? **EXCELLENT**. Now let's talk about how to turn *that* into cash.

CHAPTER 3
HOW TO TURN
YOUR IDEAS
INTO CASH

So now you know the basics when it comes to money, and you know how to dream up your own fantasy business ideas. It's time to put the two together and figure out how turn those ideas into **CASH.** Here are a few of the most important money secrets every boss needs to know to do just that. And even if you don't have big entrepreneurial plans right now, there will still be times when you can put these secrets into action. Now, this stuff might seem basic, but these are things lots of *grown-ups* don't understand properly!! So listen carefully – we're going straight into the big stuff …

MAKING MONEYYYY

In business, **PROFIT** is the money you *really* make. Your fantasy business could bring in a gazillion pounds but if your costs are *two* gazillion, you're not making a profit. That's a **LOSS.**

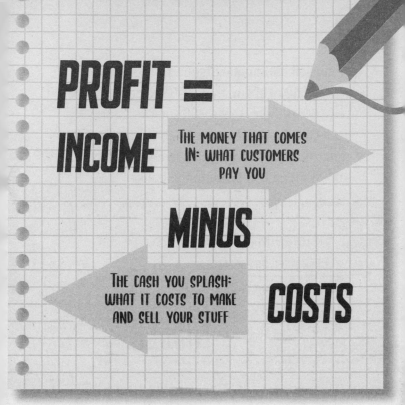

PROFIT =

INCOME
The money that comes in: what customers pay you

MINUS

The cash you splash: what it costs to make and sell your stuff

COSTS

That little calculation above depends on three ingredients:

1. THE PRICE YOU CHARGE
2. THE NUMBER OF SALES YOU MAKE
3. YOUR COSTS

If you sell handmade greeting cards at £2 and you sell 50 of them, that's £100 income. If you sell 100 of them, that's 200 smackeroonies. If your craft materials for each card cost just 50p, that's a tidy £1.50 profit on every card. Sold 100? That's £150 profit in the bank!

For the maths lovers out there:

$$\frac{\text{£1.50 profit on each card}}{\text{£2 income from each card}} = \text{a 75\% profit margin}$$

NIIIIICE.

KER-CHINNNG

So, when you think about your **PRICE**, make sure it covers your costs! But don't be too wild. People have to be willing (and able!) to pay it too! If you charge **£1 MILLION** for a cupcake that costs you 10p to make, that's a **HUGE** profit margin but … ummm … I'm not sure you're going to sell any of those!

£1,000,000

KER-CHINNNG

BANK

Think about it: what would you need to spend to get started with your fantasy business? Can you save up for it? Can a grown-up at home lend you the cash? If you have a slime empire, you'll need things like school glue every time you whip up a batch of slime, but you *don't* need a new mat and mixing bowl each time. Those are *one-off* costs. You'll cover those over time because you're spreading them over more and more and more sales.

These are things you need to think about even if you're not running a business – like if you're setting up a bake sale to raise money for charity, for example. You need to calculate the costs of all your ingredients (including the chocolate chips you *accidentally* eat while baking!) and *then* you need to figure out how much to charge and how many cakes and cookies you need to sell!

SO NOW YOU KNOW THE BASICS BEHIND PROFIT, INCOME AND COSTS. BUT TO DO SOME PROPER PLANNING, WHAT YOU NEED IS A BUDGET.

'A WHATJET?'

'A BUDGET!'

A BUDGET = A GRAND PLAN FOR WHAT TO DO WITH YOUR CASH

For each month, you list all your **INCOME** (your money **IN**) and all your **COSTS** (your money **OUT**). The **GOAL** is to make sure you have more cash coming **IN** than you have going **OUT!**

First, you write It all out like a **PLAN**. Then you write down what *actually* happens and compare the two! So if you think you'll sell 10 of those greeting cards at £2 a pop, you'll put down £20 for **INCOME**. And 10 x 50p = £5 for costs. But **THEN** maybe your local paper features your cards and you actually sell 50 of them. **GO, YOU!** So you record *that*, compare the results and revel in your amazingness.

The key is to record *everything*. That way you know exactly how much money you have and how your business is doing. If you earn over a certain amount, you'll have to pay TAX on it too. Taxes are important because they help pay for things like emergency services, schools, hospitals, roads and parks. It's how everyone in society chips in. Some big businesses – THEY KNOW WHO THEY ARE!!! – are sneaky and find loopholes to avoid paying tax. *Don't be like them!*

Budgets aren't just for businesses. We all need them! Why don't you try making one just for you? Your **MONEY IN** might be things like pocket money or birthday money if you get any. And instead of listing *costs* for **MONEY OUT**, you list the stuff you *spend* on, and the cash you *set aside* too. Budgets can help you achieve your goals – things like saving up to buy something special or a gift for a friend or family member. Bosses know that goals are *super* important. In fact, let's talk about them ...

SETTING (AND SMASHING) YOUR GOALS

If you set up a business someday, maybe you'll have a target for the number of sales or the number of customers you want to get every month. Maybe it's a goal for how much profit you want to make by the end of year. You could even use a picture like this to track progress. Track it and **SMASH IT.** ⟶

Goal-setting is a **GREAT** habit to get into. Goals are useful for all sorts of things – you can set goals for the number of hours you want to spend playing guitar or at swimming practice, time spent reading, even the number of *compliments* you'll dish out each week. Anything, really! Just make sure your goals are really clear and realistic. They should help you **STRETCH** a little – but don't be too hard on yourself if things don't work out. All you can do is give it your best shot.

TARGET REACHED

£35

£30

£25

£20

£15

£10

£8

£4

£2

CHALLENGE: CAN YOU BOSS IT WITH A BUSINESS PLAN?

Can you write a short *business plan* for your fantasy business? Think about everything we talked about in the last chapter. What problem are you solving? What have **YOU** got to offer and why is it better than the competition? Where will you sell your stuff? What's your elevator pitch?

Now mix in the stuff we've looked at in this chapter. What's it going to cost you? What price will you charge? How much profit will you make? What are your **GOALS?** Keep it realistic but *exciting*. If you do all that – **CONGRATULATIONS,** you have a **BUSINESS PLAN! WOOHOO.**

Maybe you can show it to a grown-up and see if they'd **INVEST** in your business? That means stumping up some cash to help you get started and grow. When people invest, they spend some cash in the hope of making *more* of it. If you do well, they hope to get their money back and some extra too! So let's see. How **PERSUASIVE** is your business plan? Does it make everyone say, '**OOH I NEED A PIECE OF THAAAAT**'?

SO YOU MAKE SOME MONEY. NOW WHAT?

Back to your fantasy business. Let's imagine it's all up and running, things are going swimmingly and you make a nice profit (you clever thing, you). What do you do with all your cash? Do you:

(A) SPLASH OUT *'I'm off shopping!'*

(B) INVEST IT BACK INTO THE BUSINESS (by buying equipment or spending on training or promoting your stuff)

(C) SAVE IT FOR A RAINY DAY (because you never know when you might need it!)

Even if you answered **(A)**, hopefully there's a fair bit of **(B)** and **(C)** in there too. You'll want to invest back into your business to help it grow (and invest in your learning too!) and you definitely want to be stashing some cash away in case you need it in the future. *Good habits, people. Start early.*

THINK LIKE A BOSS

'The more you learn, the more you'll earn' –
**WARREN BUFFET, billionaire investor
nicknamed the 'Oracle of Omaha'**

So there you go. Some top money secrets that even the grown-ups have trouble following sometimes. Now, we've been talking about business, but we *all* need to be clever with our cash. Even if you're not an entrepreneur, a real **BOSS** knows that if you get hold of some money, you should make a habit of saving a bit of it. And be careful when you're spending it too. Instead of jumping in like an overexcited bunny rabbit, the key is to **STOP, THINK** and **PLAN AHEAD** If you do that, *future* you is gonna **LOVE** today's you.

Right. Enough about money secrets. There are a few other important tips and tricks every boss needs to have up their sleeve. And I've found something that might just help. See you in the next chapter!

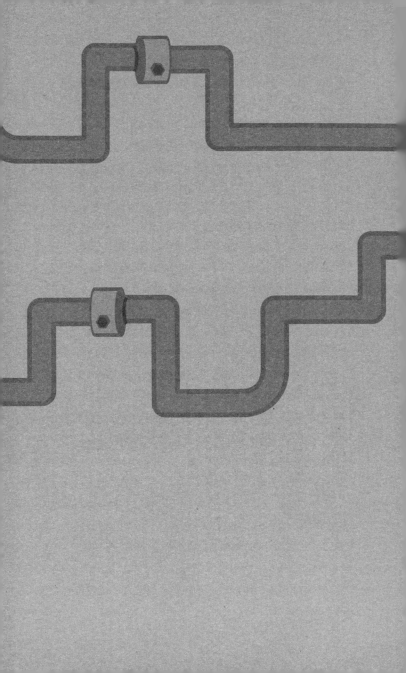

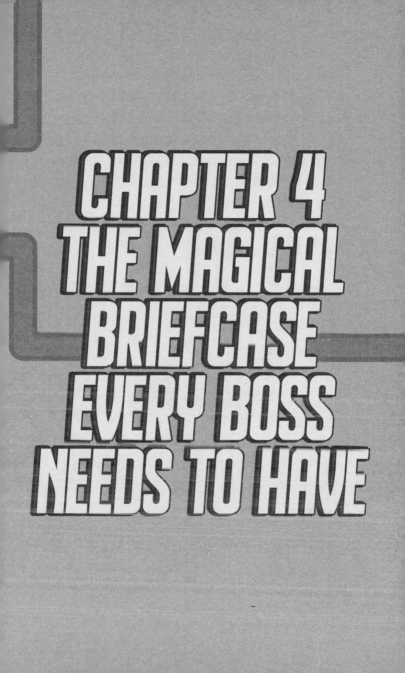

CHAPTER 4
THE MAGICAL
BRIEFCASE
EVERY BOSS
NEEDS TO HAVE

PSSST. Look what we've got here. A magical briefcase packed with potions, powers, syrups and spells that every **BOSS** needs in their toolkit. They're handy for entrepreneurs but pretty helpful in your everyday life too. And they can all be **YOURS.** Let's see what we've got in here, shall we?

OH YES...

A PROBLEM-SOLVING POTION

Problems and challenges don't faze entrepreneurs. They're like puzzles to solve, or a code to crack. That's true whether you're the boss of a soap company and can't get hold of your key ingredients (YIKES!) or whether you're trying to rebuild a LEGO spaceship but you've lost the instructions. Take on the challenge and think it through!

A SPECIAL SYRUP TO TRANSFORM MISTAKES

We often see mistakes as a bad thing. They make us feel embarrassed. Our tummies crunch, our cheeks feel hot. Know that feeling? But it doesn't have to be that way. Mistakes are an amazing way to learn and grow.

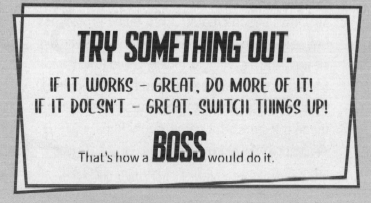

TRY SOMETHING OUT.

IF IT WORKS – GREAT, DO MORE OF IT!
IF IT DOESN'T – GREAT, SWITCH THINGS UP!

That's how a **BOSS** would do it.

TAKE TWO!
(OR ... ERR ... 5,127 ...)

Even successful entrepreneurs make mistakes. Sir James Dyson created **5,126** failed prototypes before he came up with his famous bagless vacuum cleaner. And a gaming company called Rovio made 51 games over eight years and nearly lost all their money and went bankrupt before they made the smash-hit game *Angry Birds*. We just see the shiny success story at the end, but the **PATH TO SUCCESS**

MUSEUM OF FAILURE

IS OFTEN LONG AND BUMPY AND FULL OF MISTAKES !

In Sweden, there's a whole *Museum of Failure*. It **CELEBRATES** mistakes by showcasing failed products from around the world so we can all learn from them. It's got everything from purple ketchup and inflatable sofas to magnetic sunglasses. (You have to stick magnets on your face in order to wear them. *Ummm, no thank you?!*) Maybe you can make your own mini museum to collect your mistakes. Celebrate them. Learn from them. And when you achieve your goals, whatever they are, you can look back at those mistakes and smile because you **DID IT**. You got there in the end!

YOU HOLD ON TO THAT. LET'S SEE WHAT ELSE IS IN THIS BRIEFCASE.

A SPELL TO STRETCH AND LEARN AND GROW

Entrepreneurs are curious about the world. They ask questions. They **READ** lots. They're always learning new things and seeking out exciting new opportunities. And they're not afraid to ask for help from *mentors*. Mentors are like coaches. They don't give you all the answers **(YOU CHEEKY!)** but they do give you the tools you need to find your own. And they believe in you and bring out the best in you.

I don't need to tell *you* to be curious, ask questions and read lots. But can you find any mentors of your own? Maybe a parent, guardian or teacher. Or even someone at school! Anyone you can learn from and bounce ideas with.

THINK LIKE A BOSS

'*Everything is true until it's not — the world was flat before it was round! So it's important to keep open-minded and curious. Question everything around you, and don't accept that things just "are" — ask why they are, and if they should be that way*' – **SOPHIE DEEN, founder of kids' coding company Bright Little Labs and author of Agent Asha, illustrated by Anjan Sarkar**

AN EMPATHY ELIXIR

Empathy is being able to put yourself in someone else's shoes, feel what they feel and see the world through their eyes. The best businesses do this ALL THE TIME. People who design apps, websites and all kinds of products spend ages stepping into their customers' worlds …

WHAT DO THEY REALLY NEED? WHAT DO THEY WANT?
WHAT WILL DRIVE THEM UP THE WALL?
HOW WILL THEY USE THIS PRODUCT?
HOW DOES THAT MAKE THEM FEEL?
WHAT WILL CONFUSE THEM?
WHAT WILL WOW THEM?

Sometimes the whizzes at the design company IDEO *literally* WALK in other people's shoes. OK, fine, they don't actually borrow their shoes, but they'll do things like visit stores they don't know much about and don't feel comfortable in. That way, they can understand how it feels for someone who *doesn't* cycle to walk into a bike shop, for example. Then they use *that* understanding to make the bike shop experience even better!

Walking in someone else's shoes and seeing the world from their eyes isn't just a business skill. It's a LIFE skill. For example, you might think going out for a film would be really fun, but maybe your friend is upset about something and needs some quiet time and someone to listen to them. If you can use empathy to understand how someone else is feeling and what it is they need, you can be a better friend and a better person too!

RIGHT. WHAT ELSE HAVE WE GOT IN THIS BRIEFCASE?

A SPARKLY SPRINKLING OF SCRAPPINESS

As we said earlier, savvy entrepreneurs are scrappy or *resourceful*. They know how to make do with what they have. They make things **STRETCH.** Some of the most well-known companies today started out in *garages* – from Apple and Google to Barbie doll-maker Mattel and luxury motorcycle company Harley Davidson. Nike started *in the trunk of a car.* **I KNOW.** Amazing.

You can be scrappy too. Help a grown-up rustle up some lunch with just a few ingredients. Plan

the **BEST** day out, spending as little money as possible – ideally **ZERO.** Sometimes we need to be especially careful with money. It might be because things are hard at the moment or it might be because you're saving up for something. Being resourceful can help a **LOT.**

FOCUS OF THE CLOAK

Slip into this cloak and pull that hood down (!) to become **LASER FOCUSED.** Instead of trying to do a zillion things in an OK-ish way, entrepreneurs often focus on doing **ONE** key thing and smashing it. That's what Jan Koum did when he created a mobile messaging app called WhatsApp. He focused on the simple and powerful idea of people being able to send messages over the internet. In 2014, that company was sold to Facebook for **$19 BILLION.**

THINK LIKE A BOSS

'Do one thing and do it well' – **JAN KOUM, co-founder of WhatsApp**

YEP. FOCUS.

You can use **LASER FOCUS MODE** to get rid of distractions and give all your attention to anything you're doing. Because whether you're playing football, figuring out a maths sum or painting a picture, focus means you can be at your very best! And who wouldn't want **THAT?!**

I THINK THAT'S EVERYTHING IN THE BRIEFCASE. ACTUALLY, NO, HANG ON! ONE MORE THING IN HERE. THIS ONE'S AN UNUSUAL ONE. LOOK!

A TAKE-A-BREAK PERMISSION SLIP

Ahh, you know what this is about, right? It's about **KNOWING HOW TO REST AND RECHARGE.** Every *true* boss keeps this in their briefcase. Because you can be a billionaire living the high life, but if you burn out … well, that's no good, is it? **BALANCE** is important. Work your socks off but know when to hit **PAUSE** and refuel. Take a walk. Hang out with friends. Read. Play some music. *Dance.* Whatever it takes to **R E L A X.**

Got all of that? It's yours to keep and come back to whenever you need it. So let's see what you've discovered so far. You've got to grips with the basics when it comes to money, you know how to dream up a fantasy business idea *and* how to turn it into cash. You've also got some super skills to help you along the way and to smash it in everyday life too. But remember what we said in chapter 1? True bosses know money isn't everything and they're out to make a difference in the world. So let's talk about that, shall we? It's our final stop – **BOSSING IT AND DOING SOME GOOD . . .**

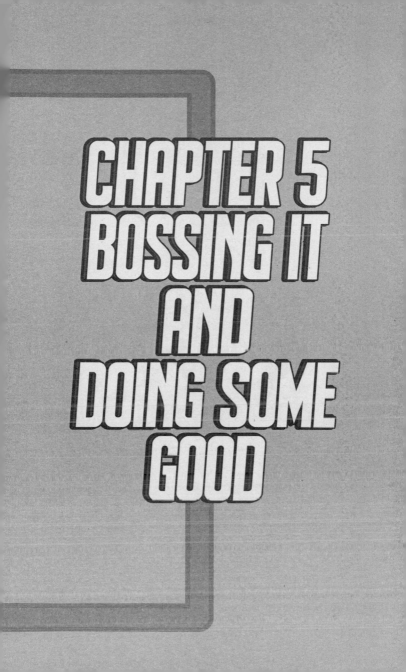

CHAPTER 5
BOSSING IT AND DOING SOME GOOD

When people think of someone who's a total **BOSS** or a super successful entrepreneur, they might imagine a self-centred villain in a suit counting wads of banknotes in their fancy office at the top of a skyscraper. But **ACTUALLY,** entrepreneurs can do a lot of good in the world. Maybe your fantasy business can too. Let's meet a few entrepreneurs who are doing just that and see if we can get those wheels turning in your imagination! Even if you *never* set up a business, you might pick up ideas for little things you could do to make the world a better place. Not just in the future but *right now*.

SO LET'S STEP INTO THE SOCIAL ENTERPRISE HALL OF FAME.

Social enterprises are businesses with goals that aren't just about *making some moneyyyy*. They're about *making a difference*. They do this in lots of ways …

DOING SOME GOOD

Take Faye Savory, who created BearHugs, a 'hug-in-a-box' gift box company, because she knew how much a care package brightened up her day when she was struggling with her chronic illness. Or Tracy Rabi, who set up Kids Finance with Tracy in Tanzania when she was *ten years old* because she realised children need to grow up knowing how to manage their money! Or Aimée Felone and David Stevens, who set up the children's publishing company Knights Of because they felt that other publishers just weren't inclusive enough and they wanted to focus on making brilliant books with authors and illustrators from *all kinds* of backgrounds.

They all saw a **NEED** and a **GAP**, and they **JUMPED RIGHT INTO ACTION.** Can *you* do that? Not just in business, but in everyday life. If you see that someone needs something, can you find a way to help? Make a card to cheer up a friend or family member who is having a hard time? Raise awareness about an issue you care about? There are **SO** many ways to do some good in the world.

LIFTING PEOPLE UP

Zakia Moulaoui's business, Invisible Cities, trains people who have been through homelessness to be city tour guides who can create and deliver their own tours to make money. *The Big Issue* is a magazine that tackles poverty by giving its sellers a chance to be 'micro-entrepreneurs', selling magazines and making a profit. These sellers are people who are homeless, or people who don't have a job and/or are really struggling financially, so this opportunity makes such a big difference. This is the amazing thing about businesses like these – they all help people who have been let down by society by giving them the tools and space they need to shine.

See, real bosses give *others* space to boss it too. Can you think of ways you can support and encourage the people around you? And help bring out the best in them the way they hopefully bring out the best in you?

THINK LIKE A BOSS

'If I can do it, you can do it, and anyone can do it'
– GITANJALI RAO, young scientist and inventor, named *TIME* magazine's Kid of the Year in 2020

KEEPING IT GREEN

Some businesses are all about greening up and protecting our planet. Like Infarm, which makes indoor 'vertical farms' to grow herbs and vegetables in restaurants, supermarkets and even in schools. They use zero harmful chemicals and, compared to other farming methods, they save massively on space, water and transport emissions. Or companies like Arthur Huang and Jarvis Liu's Miniwiz in Taiwan, which *upcycles* all SORTS of rubbish – they can transform:

👍 **OLD CLOTHES INTO RUGS**

👍 **OLD SNEAKER SOLES, CANS AND COFFEE CUPS INTO FURNITURE**

👍 **PLASTIC WASTE INTO CHEAP BUT STRONG BRICKS TO BUILD ACTUAL BUILDINGS**

And check out the companies helping to tackle our food waste mountains! Like Kromkommer in the Netherlands, which rescues wonky fruits and vegetables and whizzes them into soups! Think about that next time you come across some perfectly *imperfect* fruit and veg!

YOUR TURN!

Look around you. What challenges can you spot in the world? Can you think of a cause *you'd* want to support? Some good *you* could do?

Can you think of a fantasy business idea that could save our planet? Or maybe, one day, like the inventors we talked about, you could come up with some exciting inventions that change (and even save!) lives?

No pressure though. Start small. Could you do a spot of upcycling at home? Take something that people might throw away and magic it into something **AMAZING?** Can you get some friends on board too and make a pact to spread some good?

JUST THINK.

YOUR ACTIONS

ACTUALLY

HAVE THE POWER TO CHANGE

THE WORLD.

OR A SMALL CORNER OF IT AT LEAST.

THAT'S HUGE.

THAT'S WORTH REMEMBERING.

WHAT NOW?

Phew. That was a really high-speed tour of everything to do with mastering money secrets and building a total **BOSS MINDSET**. How are you feeling? Ready to take on the world? To get creative and follow in the footsteps of some of these entrepreneurial legends?

LILY BORN

OMARI MCQUEEN

YOU!

You now know the basics of business and being clever with your money. **AND** you know there are **SOOOO MANY** ways you can turn your awesome ideas into cash while doing some actual real good in the world. But most of all, hopefully, you've learnt how to **THINK LIKE A BOSS**.

You've got a 'magical briefcase' packed with tips and tricks every savvy entrepreneur needs in their toolkit – but these are seriously useful for *everyday life* as well. You can spot problems and get to the bottom of them. You can turn them over in your brain and figure out how to solve them. You know how to *test* things. You know how to *focus.* You can make mistakes – maybe even lots of them – and learn and grow and make something really amazing. And you know how to make a difference to our planet and the people around you, not just in the future but right now too.

HOW YOU USE THIS STUFF… WELL, THAT BIT'S UP TO YOU.

Maybe you'll use it to think up ways to raise money for a cause you care about, or to make some extra cash to buy those sneakers or that video game you've got your eye on. Maybe you'll use the skills and secrets we talked about to *level up* no matter what you're up to, whether that's at home, on a sports field, on the dance floor or at school. You might even have **BIG ENTREPRENEURIAL DREAMS!** I mean, **WHY NOT?** Everyone has to start somewhere. And you don't have to wait until some magical future to start being a **BOSS** at life. You've got everything you need to do that *right this moment*.

Happy
World Book Day!

WORLD
**BOOK
DAY**
3 MARCH 2022

As a charity, our mission is to encourage every child and young person to enjoy reading, and to have a book of their own.

Everyone is a reader — that includes you!

Whether you enjoy **comics**, **fact books**, **adventure stories**, **recipes** – books are for everyone and every book counts.

On **World Book Day**, everyone comes together to have **FUN** reading. Talking about and sharing books with your friends and family makes reading even more memorable and magic.

World Book Day® is a registered charity sponsored by National Book Tokens.

Illustration by Allen Fatimaharan © 2021

WORLD
BOOK DAY
3 MARCH 2022

Where will your **reading journey** take you next?

1 Take a trip to your local bookshop

Brimming with brilliant books and helpful booksellers to share awesome reading recommendations, bookshops are magical places. You can even enjoy booky events and meet your favourite authors and illustrators!

Find your nearest bookseller at **booksaremybag.com/Home**

2 Join your local library

A world awaits you in your local library – that place where all the books you could ever want to read awaits. Even better, you can borrow them for **FREE**! Libraries can offer expert advice on what to read next, as well as free family reading events.

Find your local library at **gov.uk/local-library-services**

Scan here to visit our website!

3 Check out the World Book Day website

Looking for reading tips, advice and inspiration? There is so much to discover at worldbookday.com/getreading, packed with book recommendations, fun activities, audiobooks, and videos to enjoy on your own or as a family, as well as competitions and all the latest book news galore.

World Book Day® is a registered charity sponsored by National Book Tokens

NATIONAL **BOOK** tokens

Illustration by Allen Fatimaharan © 2021